God's

Revelations

About You

Today

Revised Edition

By: Larry L. Scaglione

PRESS

God's Revelations About You Today
by Larry L. Scaglione

Printed in the United States of America

Library of Congress Control Number: 2003097232
ISBN 9781612153506

www.xulonpress.com

Dedication

I dedicate this book to God who is my Heavenly Father, to Jesus Christ who is my personal Lord and Savior, to God's indwelling Holy Spirit who guided me regarding it's contents, and to my wonderful wife Portia who is my most cherished gift from God.

All of the credit for the creation of this book belongs to my Heavenly Father who led me to write it for your edification.

Table of Contents

Acknowledgements

First I want to acknowledge God who lead me through His indwelling Holy Spirit to write this book for you, because without His encouragement it would not have been written or published.

I would like to acknowledge and thank Irina Knox, and Michael Dante for editing the manuscript for this edition of God's Revelations about you. They enhanced this book greatly through their dedicated and tireless work on it.

All scripture referenced in this book has been taken from the Comparative Study Bible with permission from the Zondervan Publishing House.

Introduction

This book contains God's documented revelations that apply to you today. Many of these revelations have remained obscure biblical truths until now. It is finally time for them to be revealed to you for your personal edification.

If I were limited to just one book that would explain the mysteries that God has established regarding my life here on earth, this would be that book. In chapter 2, it reveals who God says you are. In chapter 3, it explains why you are here. Chapter 9, reveals God's plan for you. Chapter 11, reveals what God wants from you today, and in chapter 13, it reveals a method of praying that the bible teaches will be answered. This book has been written to explain these obscure biblical teachings in a very clear and simple manner.

Chapter 1

God's Revelations about you

The following chapters in this book contain revelations in the bible that have been written specifically to you. They are being published in this book in an effort to make them more readily available for you. They reveal biblical mysteries about your life including why you are here, what you can expect to go through in this life, the spiritual battle that (you are) involved in, and much more. This book is being written for you in an effort to give you a better understanding of the circumstances regarding your life, according to the scriptures documented in the bible.

As you read this book I encourage you to refer to your own bible in order to verify the contents of this book for yourself. I personally use the Comparative Study Bible published by Zondervan and would highly recommend this bible to you if you don't already own one. The Comparative Study Bibles have four different translations of each bible verse in them. I like to use it because you can compare four different translations of the same verse side by side in one book. After you compare four different translations of each verse you will gain a better understanding of the message in it.

For those of you who are not able to obtain a bible for yourself, I have included the four bible translations that I personally use in this book for you.

I also recommend the NIV Topical Study Bible which Zondervan also publishes. It will enable you to look up the appropriate scripture for almost any subject.

Chapter 2

Who God says you are

G od says that you are His son or His daughter, not a servant who follows his or her master, or a sheep who follows his or her Sheppard, but (His son or His daughter). Your relationship to God is a very personal relationship. The knowledge and understanding that you are a child of God's can and will be a life changing experience for some of you. If you are living a life right now that you know is not appropriate, the realization that you are God's son or His daughter should give you the motivation to start making some changes in the way that you are currently living. If you are not already aware of your relationship to God, or don't actually believe that you are God's son or His daughter, after reading this chapter you will.

Once you have come to the realization that you have been born (created) to be one of God's own children, this awareness of your importance in this world should give you the motivation to start making some changes in your life. Start living and treating yourself according to who you really are. You are a child of God's and you should make any changes in your life that are necessary to start living like one.

The bible teaches in (Romans 8:15,16) below, that when you accept Jesus Christ as your personal Lord and Savior, (you will become a child of God's). This is accomplished when God places His Holy Spirit (Who is also called The Spirit of Adoption) in you.

King James Version - (Romans 8:15,16), For ye have not received the spirit of bondage to fear; but ye have received the Spirit of adoption, whereby we cry, Abba, Father. (16), The Spirit itself beareth witness with our spirit, that we are the children of God.

Amplified Version - (Romans 8:15,16), For [the Spirit which] you have now received [is] not a spirit of slavery to put you once more in bondage to fear, but you have received the Spirit of adoption - the Spirit producing sonship - in [the bliss of] which we cry, Abba! [That is] Father! (16), The

Spirit Himself [thus] testifies together with our own spirit, [assuring us] that we are children of God.

New American Standard Version - (Romans 8:15,16), For you have not received a spirit of slavery leading to fear again, but you have received a spirit of adoption as sons by which we cry, "Abba! Father!" (16), The Spirit Himself bears witness with our spirit that we are children of God.

New International Version - (Romans 8:15,16), for you did not receive a spirit that makes you a slave again to fear, but you received the Spirit of sonship. And by Him we cry, "Abba, Father," (16), The Spirit Himself testifies with our spirit that we are God's children.

If you are still not convinced that you are a child of God's, the bible clearly reveals that you are in (1 John 3:1,2) below.

King James Version - (1 John 3:1,2), Behold, what manner of love the Father hath bestowed upon us, that we should be called the sons of God: therefore the world knoweth us not, because it knew Him not. (2), Beloved, now are we the sons of God, and it doth not yet appear what we shall be: but we know that, when He shall appear, we shall be like Him; for we shall see him as He is.

Amplified Version - (1 John 3:1,2), See what [an incredible] quality of love the Father has given (shown, bestowed on) us, that we should [be permitted to] be named and called and counted the children of God! And so we are! The reason that the world does not know (recognize, acknowledge) us, is that it does not know (recognize, acknowledge) Him. (2), Beloved, we are [even here and] now God's children; it is not yet disclosed (made clear) what we shall be [hereafter], but we know that when He comes and is manifested we shall [as God's children] resemble and be like Him, for we shall see Him, just as He [really] is.

New American Standard Version - (1 John 3:1,2), See how great a love the Father has bestowed upon us, that we should be called children of God; and such we are. For this reason the world does not know us, because it did not know Him. (2), Beloved, now we are children of God, and it has not appeared as yet what we shall be. We know that, when He appears, we shall be like Him, because we shall see Him just as He is.

New International Version - (1 John 3:1,2), How great is the love the Father has lavished on us, that we should be called children of God! and that is what we are! The reason the world does not know us is that it did not know Him. (2),

Dear friends, now we are children of God, and what we will be has not yet been made known. But we know that when He appears, we shall be like Him, for we shall see Him as He is.

There isn't any room for misunderstanding God's Word in (2 Corinthians 6:18) below. In this verse God, through the apostle Paul reveals to you that He is your Father and you are His child.

King James Version - (2 Corinthians 6:18), "And I will be a Father unto you, and ye shall be My sons and daughters," saith the Lord Almighty.

Amplified Version - (2 Corinthians 6:18), "And I will be a Father to you, and you shall be My sons and daughters," says the Lord Almighty.

New American Standard Version - (2 Corinthians 6:18), "And I will be a Father to you, and you shall be sons and daughters to Me," Says the Lord Almighty.

New International Version - (2 Corinthians 6:18),"I will be a Father to you, and you will be My sons and daughters," says the Lord Almighty.

Chapter 3

Why are you here?

One reason that you are here, and probably the most important reason that God put you here on earth is to develop the character of Christ in you. This will be revealed to you in the following pages of this chapter. You will develop this character by observing others, and also from your own personal experiences that the consequences for living a sinful life bring only physical or mental pain and suffering.

When you observe someone else living a sin filled life, you are able to see the negative consequences that sin has produced in that person's life. This is one way in which you will see for yourself the results of sinning. You will grow in character through each of these experiences.

Another way that you grow in character each day is by overcoming the temptations in your own life to sin. By overcoming these daily temptations over a lifetime you will actually change inwardly, and you will gradually develop in character throughout the course of your life. Even if you give in to the temptations to sin, you will still grow in character by experiencing the negative consequence that sin produces. You will learn from your personal experiences and grow in character whether you choose to sin or not. This paradox reveals that God has made it impossible for you not to grow in character through your personal experiences here on earth.

If you will take a close look at the Amplified version of (Romans 8:29) below, you will see the words (and share inwardly His likeness). This verse is revealing to you that you are here to develop the character of Christ. God has predestined you before you were even born to be molded inwardly (in character) to the image of Christ, so that Jesus will become the first born among many brethren, (meaning brothers and sisters), and you are included among those brothers and sisters.

Amplified Version - (Romans 8:29), for those whom He foreknew - of whom He was aware and loved beforehand - He also destined from the beginning (foreordaining them) to be molded into the image of His Son [and share inwardly His likeness], that He might become the first-born among many brethren.

God has left nothing to chance, in order to assure that you are conformed inwardly into the character of Christ. God even places His Holy Spirit in you to insure that you develop in character while you are here. The bible reveals this for you in (Ezekiel 36:27) below.

King James Version - (Ezekiel 36:27), "And I will put My Spirit within you, and cause you to walk in My statutes, and ye shall keep My judgments, and do them."

Amplified Version - (Ezekiel 36:27), "And I will put My Spirit within you and cause you to walk in My statutes, and you shall heed My ordinances, and do them."

New American Standard Version - (Ezekiel 36:27), "And I will put My Spirit within you and cause you to walk in My statutes, and you will be careful to observe My ordinances."

New International Version - (Ezekiel 36:27), "And I will put My Spirit in you and move you to follow My decrees and be careful to keep My laws."

By reading the information in this chapter, you should have become aware that the reason that you are here on earth is to develop the character of Christ in you. God has assured that you will grow in character regardless of the choices that you make. He has also placed His Holy Spirit in you to guide and help you to achieve His purpose in your life.

It is important that you know what the character traits of Christ are so that you can recognize the situations in your daily life that enable you to develop them. This will add an entirely new dimension and fascination to the complexities of the tests, trials, temptations and situations that God has arranged for you to encounter. It will also change and enhance the way you perceive each situation that you encounter. You will be able to recognize a test, trial, temptation or situation in your life for what it really is, an opportunity to develop one or more of the character traits of Christ in you.

The next time you are held up by traffic or delayed in a line at a cash register, you will be able to identify either of these situations as a test, trial, or situation designed by God to develop patience and self control, instead of a random situation and inconvenience to you. Patience and self control are two of the character traits that you are here to develop. Instead of getting angry when you are delayed, you will be able to remain calm knowing that the delay is not a random inconvenience, but a deliberate test, trial, or situation designed to develop your character. This situation analysis will reveal to you the degree to which God is involved in your daily life. When you recognize the complexities and purpose of the tests, trials, temptations and situations in you life, in addition to the fact that God placed His Holy Spirit in you to guide you, He won't seem so far away anymore.

In the Amplified Version of (1 Corinthians 10:13) below, it is revealed to you that God will not allow the temptations and trials that you encounter, to be more than you can bear.

Amplified Version - (1 Corinthians 10:13), For no temptation - no trial regarded as enticing to sin [no matter how it comes or where it Leads] - has overtaken you and laid hold on you that is beyond human resistance and that is not adjusted and adopted and belonging to human experience, and such as man can bear. But God is faithful [to His word and to His compassionate nature], and He [can be trusted] not to let you be tempted and tried and assayed beyond

your ability and strength of resistance and power to endure,

but with the temptation He will [always] provide the way

out - the means of escape to a landing place - that you may

be capable and strong and powerful patiently to bear up

under it.

You will need to become familiar with the character traits revealed in (Galatians 5:22,23) below in order to identify which character trait or traits are being developed in you by the situations that you encounter. This will also allow you to remain calm and have more self control in the situations that you encounter. It will enable you to benefit much more by recognizing and understanding the process of character development that you are going through.

The bible reveals that when God places His Holy Spirit in you, He will develop the character traits in you that He wants all Christians (His children) to develop here on earth. These character traits are referred to in the bible as (the fruit of the Spirit) and they are; love, joy, peace, patience, kindness, goodness, faithfulness, gentleness and self-control.

New International Version - (Galatians 5:22,23), But the fruit of the Spirit is love, joy, peace, patience, kindness, goodness, faithfulness, (23), gentleness and self-control. Against such things there is no law.

Chapter 4

The Spiritual Battle Involving You

O nce you have read this chapter you will realize that there is a spiritual battle going on that does involve you, and that you have been given the power and authority by God to win it. This battle is recorded in the bible, and has been documented in this chapter for you. After you have accepted Jesus Christ as your Lord and Savior you will have authority over the power of all the spiritual influences in your life. The bible reveals this to you in (Luke 10:19) below.

King James Version - (Luke 10:19), "Behold, I give unto you power to tread on serpents and scorpions, and over all the power of the enemy: and nothing shall by any means hurt you."

Amplified Version - (Luke 10:19), "Behold! I have given you authority and power to trample upon serpents and scorpions, and (physical and mental strength and ability) over all the power that the enemy [possess], and nothing shall in any way harm you."

New American Standard Version - (Luke 10:19), "Behold, I have given you authority to tread upon serpents and scorpions, and over all the power of the enemy, and nothing shall injure you."

New International Version - (Luke 10:19), "I have given you authority to trample on snakes and scorpions and to overcome all the power of the enemy; nothing will harm you."

Spiritual influences are very subtle in nature. Unless you become aware that spiritual influences do affect your life, you will never realize that they may be the source of the problems in your life. If you are currently dabbling in the occult for example, and fill that you are not in control of what is taking place as a direct result of your actions you are right. You are subjecting yourself to the influence of spiritual beings who can have a devastating influence and impact on your life.

If you find yourself giving in to the same temptations day after day it's because your temptations may be the result of spiritual influences which can have a profound influence on your thoughts and behavior. If you find yourself addicted to drugs, alcohol, or pornography, these are all addictions that can be the end result of spiritual influence. When you recognize that the reason that you can't break free of these addictions could possibly be spiritual influences, then you can actually use this knowledge to your advantage.

The bible reveals in (Ephesians 6:12) below, that we wrestle against spiritual forces of evil. Do not be frightened by them though. You will discover as you read this book that God has placed restrictions on what He will allow them to do to you. God will only allow them to tempt or try to influence you to sin. It is through this process of resisting their temptations and influences on you to sin, that you are able to develop in character.

King James Version - (Ephesians 6:12), for we wrestle not against flesh and blood, but against principalities, against powers, against the rulers of the darkness of this world, against spiritual wickedness in high places.

Amplified Version - (Ephesians 6:12), For we are not wrestling with flesh and blood - contending only with physical opponents - but against the despotisms, against the powers, against [the master spirits who are] the world rulers of this present darkness, against the spirit forces of wickedness in the heavenly (supernatural) sphere.

New American Standard Version - (Ephesians 6:12), For our struggle is not against flesh and blood, but against the rulers, against the powers, against the world forces of this darkness, against the spiritual forces of wickedness in the heavenly places.

New International Version - (Ephesians 6:12), for our struggle is not against flesh and blood, but against the rulers, against the authorities, against the powers of this dark world and against the spiritual forces of evil in the heavenly realms.

Movies today like to depict demons with the ability to hurt what they want you to believe are defenseless Christians, and throw Priests across the room when they try unsuccessfully to rebuke them. The bible reveals to you in (Luke 10:19), which you discovered earlier in this chapter that God gives not only Priests, but you as well, the authority and power to successfully bind and rebuke demons in the name of Jesus Christ. Demons are powerless to disobey a verbal command given to them in the Name of Jesus Christ, whether it is by a Priest or by you. It is written that every knee shall bow before the Lord, and that includes demons as well. They are no match for the power and authority that Jesus Christ has over them.

Once you have been saved, you will have God's Holy Spirit in you as revealed to you in (Ezekiel 36:27), in chapter 3. God's Spirit is certainly more powerful than the devil and all of the demons put together. Actually the devil and his demons are completely powerless against God, and they are also not able to stand up to the power and authority of Jesus Christ. That is why we are able to bind and rebuke demons when we do it in the name of Jesus Christ.

Chapter 5

Who are the Devil and the Demons?

T he devil and the demons are nothing more than angels or spiritual beings that were cast out of heaven and down to earth for turning against God. According to the bible, God allows the demons to tempt and influence us with lust, greed, and the desire for power and for financial gains. Pursuing these desires ultimately results in living unrighteous lives, and exhibiting unethical behavior as well as a callus and total disregard for others. Unfortunately these unethical people find that they end up alone, and are left at the end of their lives with only shame, and regret. At that point they also realize that all of the money and possessions that they acquired, often at the expense of others, were not in any way equal to what they had given up in exchange for them. Unfortunately for many it will be too late to reverse the course of the life they had chosen to live. These experiences are repeated over and over again by many people here on earth, in order to teach them through their own personal experiences that a sinful and unethical life style only produces tragedy, shame, emptiness and unhappiness. This is one way that God allows us to develop our character as individuals, by allowing each of us to experience the consequences of sin for ourselves here on earth.

For those who do resist these temptations, the result is an immediate strengthening and growth in their character. This process is similar to the physical benefits of working out at a gym. In a gym you have to exert resistance against weights in order to develop strong mussels. The same principle applies when you exert resistance against temptations, except you strengthen your character instead of your muscles.

In (Ezekiel 28:14,15) below, the bible reveals that the devil was once an anointed cherub (guardian angle), in heaven. It also reveals that in spite of the fact that God created him righteous, over time the devil eventually became wicked.

King James Version - (Ezekiel 28:14,15), "Thou art the anointed cherub that covereth; and I have set thee so: thou wast upon the holy mountain of God; thou hast walked up and down in the midst of the stones of fire. (15), Thou wast perfect in thy ways from the day that thou wast created, till iniquity was found in thee."

Amplified Version - (Ezekiel 28:14,15), "You were the anointed cherub that covers with overshadowing [wings], and I set you so. You were upon the holy mountain of God; you walked up and down in the midst of the stones of fire [like the paved work of gleaming sapphire stone upon which the God of Israel walked on Mount Sinai] (15), You were blameless in your ways from the day you were created, until iniquity and guilt were found in you."

New American Standard Version - (Ezekiel 28:14,15), "You were the anointed cherub who covers, And I placed you there. You were on the holy mountain of God; You walked in the midst of the stones of fire. (15), You were blameless in your ways from the day you were created, until unrighteousness was found in you."

New International Version - (Ezekiel 28:14,15), "You were anointed as a guardian cherub, for so I ordained you. You were on the holy mount of God; you walked among the fiery stones. (15), You were blameless in your ways from the day you were created till wickedness was found in you."

The devil was not satisfied serving God. The devil wanted to place a throne for himself in heaven above the stars of God. His intentions were to acquire for himself the glory that belongs only to God. It is obvious that the devil unfortunately didn't stop to consider the fact that God who is the Creator and Ruler of the Universe, is also the creator and ruler over him. The bible reveals this for you in (Isaiah 14:13,14), below.

King James Version - (Isaiah 14:13,14), for thou hast said in thine heart, "I will ascend into heaven, I will exalt my throne above the stars of God: I will sit also upon the mount of the congregation, in the sides of the north: (14), I will ascend above the heights of the clouds: I will be like the Most High."

Amplified Version - (Isaiah 14:13,14), And you said in your heart, "I will ascend to Heaven; I will exalt my throne above the stars of God; I will sit upon the mount of assembly in the uttermost north; (14), I will ascend above the heights of the clouds, I will make myself like the Most High."

New American Standard Version - (Isaiah 14:13,14), But you said in your heart, "I will ascend to heaven; I will raise my throne above the stars of God, And I will sit on the mount of assembly in the recesses of the north. (14), I will ascend above the heights of the clouds; I will make myself like the Most High."

New International Version - (Isaiah 14:13,14), You said in your heart, "I will ascend to heaven; I will raise my throne above the stars of God; I will sit enthroned on the mount of assembly, on the utmost heights of the sacred mountain. (14), I will ascend above the tops of the clouds; I will make myself like the Most High."

The bible reveals to you in (Ezekiel 28:16-19) below, that the devil became proud because of his beauty, and he corrupted his God given wisdom because of his splendor. The devil misused his God given position and gifts in heaven, and ultimately became filled with pride and violence. As a result, God removed the devil from heaven for turning against Him.

King James Version - (Ezekiel 28:16-19), "By the multitude of thy merchandise they have filled the midst of thee with violence, and thou hast sinned: therefore I will cast thee as profane out of the mountain of God: and I will destroy thee, O covering cherub, from the midst of the stones of fire. (17), Thine heart was lifted up because of thy beauty, thou hast corrupted thy wisdom by reason of thy brightness: I will cast thee to the ground, I will lay thee before kings, that they may behold thee. (18), thou hast defiled thy sanctuaries by the multitude of thine iniquities, by the iniquity of thy traffic; therefore will I bring forth a fire from the midst of thee, it shall devour thee, and I will bring thee to ashes upon the earth in the sight of all them that behold thee. (19), All they that know thee among the people shall be astonished at thee: thou shalt be a terror, and never shalt thou be any more."

Amplified Version - (Ezekiel 28:16-19), "Through the abundance of your commerce you were filled with lawless-ness and violence, and you sinned; therefore I cast you out as a profane thing from the mountain of God, and the guardian cherub drove you out from the midst of the stones of fire. (17), Your heart was proud and lifted up because of your beauty; you corrupted your wisdom for the sake of your splendor. I cast you to the ground; I lay you before kings that they might gaze at you. (18), You have profaned your sanctuaries by the multitude of your iniquities and the enormity of your guilt, by the unrighteousness of your trade. Therefore I have brought forth a fire from your midst; it has consumed you, and I have reduced you to ashes upon the earth in the sight of all who looked at you. (19), All who know you among the people are astonished and appalled at you; you have come to a horrible end and shall never return to being."

New American Standard Version - (Ezekiel 28:16-19), "By the abundance of your trade you were internally filled with violence, and you sinned; Therefore I have cast you as profane from the mountain of God. And I have destroyed you, O covering cherub, from the midst of the stones of fire. (17), Your heart was lifted up because of your beauty; You corrupted your wisdom by reason of your splendor. I cast you to the ground; I put you before kings, That they may see you. (18), By the multitude of your iniquities, In the unrighteousness of your trade, you profaned your sanctuaries. Therefore I have brought fire from the midst of you; It has consumed you, and I have turned you to ashes on the earth in the eyes of all who see you. (19), All who know you among the peoples are appalled at you; You have become terrified, and you will be no more."

New International Version - (Ezekiel 28:16-19), "Through your widespread trade you were filled with violence, and you sinned. So I drove you in disgrace from the mount of God, and I expelled you, O guardian cherub, from among the fiery stones. (17), Your heart became proud on account of your beauty, and you corrupted your wisdom because of your splendor. So I threw you to the earth; I made a spectacle of you before kings. (18), By your many sins and dishonest trade you have desecrated your sanctuaries. So I made a fire come out of you, and it consumed you, and I reduced you to ashes on the ground in the sight of all who were watching. (19), All the nations who knew you are appalled at you; you have come to a horrible end and will be no more."

The devil along with the angels who followed him, mis-used their God given free will and chose to turn against God who created them. It is documented in (Revelation 12:7-9) of the bible, that God through Michael and His loyal angels removed the devil and all who followed him from heaven in a fierce battle.

King James Version - (Revelation 12:7-9), And there was war in heaven: Michael and his angels fought against the dragon; and the dragon fought his angels (8), And prevailed not; neither was their place found any more in heaven. (9), And the great dragon was cast out, that old serpent, called the Devil, and Satan, which deceiveth the whole world: he was cast out into the earth, and his angels were cast out with him.

Amplified Version - (Revelation 12:7-9), Then war broke out in heaven, Michael and his angels going forth to battle with the dragon; and the dragon and his angels fought (8), But they were defeated and there was no room found for them in heaven any longer. (9), And the huge dragon was cast down and out, that ages-old serpent, who is called the Devil and Satan, he who is the seducer (deceiver) of all humanity the world over; he was forced out and down to the earth, and his angels were flung out along with him.

New American Standard Version - (Revelation 12:7-9), And there was war in heaven, Michael and his angels waging war with the dragon. And the dragon and his angels waged war, (8), and they were not strong enough, and there was no longer a place found for them in heaven. (9), And the great dragon was thrown down, the serpent of old who is called the devil and Satan, who deceives the whole world; he was thrown down to the earth, and his angels were thrown down with him.

New International Version - (Revelation 12:7-9), And there was war in heaven. Michael and his angels fought against the dragon, and the dragon and his angels fought back. (8), But he was not strong enough, and they lost their place in heaven. (9), The great dragon was hurled down - that ancient serpent called the devil, or Satan, who leads the whole world astray. He was hurled to the earth, and his angels with him.

The verses above reveal the betrayal of God by the devil and the demons as well as the place that God exiled them to. According to the bible in the verses above they are now here on earth with us. Being aware of this fact is very important to each of us because it has a direct impact on our lives.

In addition to being removed from heaven, the devil and the demons have no chance of regaining their angelic positions because of their actions. They are aware of the fact that if they can successfully tempt or influence you to turn to a sinful life and away from God, then you won't be able to enter heaven either. This may seem like a petty and spiteful attitude for them to have, but obviously according to the bible it is the one that they have chosen to take concerning us. They were created by God as spiritual beings (angels), to serve not only God, but also us as God's children. Unlike the loyal angles in heaven, the demons arrogantly consider themselves better that you and I because they were created as Angelic Spiritual beings, and not mere human beings like you and I who were created way down here on earth. Anyway, This is their reasoning for initiating this spiritual battle with you and I. They resent the fact that we who were created as mere human beings will eventually reside in heaven as God's children, who will judge angles. This personal encounter with demons here on earth will be revealed and explained in detail for you in the next chapter.

Chapter 6

What can the Devil and the Demons do to you?

The devil and the demons will try to tempt and influence you many times each day. This process of being tempted is revealed for you in the bible so that you will be prepared to deal with it. All men and women are temped as they go through their lives here on earth, not just you. This process of resisting and overcoming temptations in your life is what facilitates the building of your character while you are here. The bible reveals this process for you in (1 Corinthians 10:11-13) below. The bible also reveals for you that God will not allow you to be tempted beyond what you can bear.

King James Version - (1 Corinthians 10:11-13), Now all these things happened unto them for examples: and they are written for our admonition, upon whom the ends of the world are come. (12), Wherefore let him that thinketh he standeth take heed lest he fall. (13), There hath no temptation taken you but such as is common to man: but God is faithful, who will not suffer you to be tempted above that ye are able; but will with the temptation also make a way to escape, that ye may be able to bear it.

Amplified Version - (1 Corinthians 10:11-13), Now these things befell them by way of a figure - as an example and warning [to us]; they were written to admonish and fit us for right action by good instruction, we in whose days the ages have reached their climax - their consummation and concluding period. (12), Therefore let any one who thinks he stands - who feels sure that he has a steadfast mind and is standing firm - take heed lest he fall [into sin]. (13), For no temptation - no trial regarded as enticing to sin [no matter how it comes or where it leads] - has overtaken you and laid hold on you that is beyond human resistance and that is not adjusted and adapted and belonging to human experience, and such as man can bear. But God is faithful [to His word and to His compassionate nature], and He [can be trusted] not to let you be tempted and tried and assayed beyond your ability and strength of resistance and power to endure, but with the temptation He will [always] provide the way out - the means of escape to a landing place - that you may be capable and strong and powerful patiently to bear up under it.

New American Standard Version - (1 Corinthians 10:11-13), Now these things happened to them as an example, and they were written for our instruction, upon whom the ends of the ages have come. (12), Therefore let him who thinks he stands take heed lest he fall. (13), No temptation has over-taken you but such as is common to man; and God is faithful, who will not allow you to be tempted beyond what you are able, but with the temptation will provide the way of escape also, that you may be able to endure it.

New International Version - (1 Corinthians 10:11-13), These things happened to them as examples and were written down as warnings for us, on whom the fulfillment of the ages has come. (12), So, if you think you are standing firm, be careful that you don't fall! (13), No temptation has seized you except what is common to man. And God is faithful; He will not let you be tempted beyond what you can bear. But when you are tempted, he will also provide a way out so that you can stand up under it.

I hope that you were made aware by (1 Corinthians 10:11-13) above, that God has assured your success in this life. These verses reveal that God will always provide a way out of a temptation for you.

These temptations and influences vary in their importance and in their intensity. Most of them have the same common goal which is to drive you as far away from a Godly life as possible. These temptations range from temptations of the flesh, to using drugs and alcohol, which will have a negative influence on a person's life. They bring instant gratification to you, while they slowly destroy your character and your life at the same time. Your initial temptation will seem harmless enough, but it will serve as a springboard to other temptations which will have more severe affects on your life. As time goes by, you will become aware that all of these temptations have had a devastating effect on your life. At that point it is easy to believe that it's too late to do anything about it, but it is never too late to start changing your life.

Chapter 7

Why the Devil and Demons are bothering you

The devil and the demons are trying to influence you through daily temptations to turn to a sinful life and away from God. They don't want you to inherit the kingdom of God in heaven. They will continuously try to get you to turn to a sinful life. Their goal is to get you to turn away from God, and be weeded out of God's kingdom as they were. They were weeded out of heaven for turning against God, and they know that if they can get you to turn away from God, then you will be weeded out too. Jesus explains this weeding out of the kingdom process in His parable of the weeds found in (Matthew 13:38-41) below.

King James Version - (Matthew 13:38-41), The field is the world; the good seed are the children of the kingdom; but the tares are the children of the wicked one; (39), The enemy that sowed them is the devil; the harvest is the end of the world; and the reapers are the angels. (40), As therefore the tares are gathered and burned in the fire; so shall it be in the end of this world. (41), The Son of man shall send forth His angels, and they shall gather out of His kingdom all things that offend, and them which do iniquity.

Amplified Version - (Matthew 13:38-41), The field is the world, and the good seed means the children of the kingdom; the darnel is the children of the evil one, (39), And the enemy who sowed it is the devil; the harvest is the close and con-summation of the age, and the reapers are angels. (40), Just as the darnel (wild wheat) is gathered and burned with fire, so it will be at the close of the age. (41), The Son of man will send forth His angels, and they will gather out of His kingdom all causes of offense - persons by who others are drawn into error or sin - and all who do iniquity and act wickedly.

New American Standard Version - (Matthew 13:38-41), and the field is the world; and as for the good seed, these are the sons of the kingdom; and the tares are the sons of the evil one; (39), and the enemy who sowed them is the devil, and the harvest is the end of the age; and the reapers are angels. (40), Therefore just as the tares are gathered up and burned with fire, so shall it be at the end of the age. (41), The Son of man will send forth His angels, and they will gather out of His kingdom all stumbling blocks, and those who commit lawlessness.

New International version - (Matthew 13:38-41), The field is the world and the good seed stands for the sons of the kingdom. The weeds are the sons of the evil one, (39), and the enemy who sows them is the devil. The harvest is the end of the age, and the harvesters are angels. (40), As the weeds are pulled up and burned in the fire, so it will be at the end of the age. (41), The Son of Man will send out His angels, and they will weed out of His kingdom everything that causes sin and all who do evil.

Jesus has already paid the penalty for all of your sins, this includes your past, present, and future sins. When Jesus gave His life on the cross, the penalty was paid in full. You do however have to claim that payment by accepting Jesus Christ as your personal Lord and Savior, and by turning away from sinful behavior, if you want His sacrifice on the cross applied to you. Once you accept Jesus Christ as your personal Lord and Savior, and reject your sinful behavior, then the devil and the demons will have at that point, lost their spiritual battle with you and with God, over where you will spend eternity. The bible teaches in (John 3:16) below, that those who believe in, and accept Jesus Christ as their personal Lord and Savior will have eternal life.

King James Version - (John 3:16), For God so loved the world, that He gave His only begotten Son, that whosoever believeth in Him should not perish, but have everlasting life.

Amplified Version - (John 3:16), For God so greatly loved and dearly prized the world that He [even] gave up His only-begotten (unique) Son, so that whoever believes in (trusts, clings to, relies on) Him shall not perish - come to destruction, be lost - but have eternal (everlasting) life.

New American Standard Version - (John 3:16), For God so loved the world, that He gave His only begotten Son, that whoever believes in Him should not perish, but have eternal life.

New International Version - (John 3:16), For God so loved the world that He gave His one and only Son, that whoever believes in Him shall not perish but have eternal life.

Chapter 8

God's Grace and You

G od's grace is His unearned, and unmerited favor in your life. By following the biblical teachings in this book you can experience God's grace in your life. The bible reveals that God's grace is not something that you can earn, or even something that you deserve. The bible reveals that God's grace is His unearned and unmerited favor in your life. It is not something that you deserve just because you go to church on Sundays or because you live a good life according to your own standards. God's Grace is a gift from Him to you because He is your father and loves you very much.

When you pray daily and start to share each day with God, life itself will take on more meaning for you, and circumstances may begin to change in your life. Some of these changes could be the direct result of your improved self-image now that you are aware that you are a child of God's. Some of the added joy that you may be experiencing could be the result of just a better attitude. It may just be a coincidence that circumstances in your life mysteriously begin to change and improve. It could be by chance that you discover that the character traits of love, joy, peace, patience, kindness, goodness, gentleness, faithfulness and self-control start to develop and reveal themselves in you. You will eventually become aware as I have, that what you are experiencing is God's grace in your life. The bible reveals in (Ephesians 2:8) below, that you are saved by God's grace through your faith.

King James Version - (Ephesians 2:8), For by grace are ye saved through faith; and that not of yourselves: It is the gift of God.

Amplified Version - (Ephesians 2:8), For it is by free grace (God's unmerited favor) that you are saved (delivered from judgment and made partakers of Christ's salvation) through [your] faith. And this [salvation] is not of yourselves - of your own doing, it came not through your own striving - but it is the gift of God.

New American Standard Version - (Ephesians 2:8), For by grace you have been saved through faith; and that not of yourselves, it is the gift of God.

New International Version - (Ephesians 2:8), For it is by grace you have been saved, through faith - and this is not from yourselves, it is the gift of God.

In spite of the life that you may be currently living, when you accept Jesus Christ as your personal Lord and Savior and repent of your sins, you will be saved by God's grace. The bible reveals to you in (Ephesians 2:1-5) below, that God will save you by His grace even while you are still living a sinful life.

King James Version - (Ephesians 2:1-5), And you hath He quickened, who were dead in trespasses and sins! (2), Wherein in time past ye walked according to the course of this world, according to the prince of the power of the air, the spirit that now worketh in the children of disobedience: (3), Among whom also we all had our conversation in times past in the lusts of our flesh, fulfilling the desires of the flesh and of the mind; and were by nature the children of wrath, even as others. (4), But God, who is rich in mercy, for His great love wherewith He loved us, (5), Even when we were dead in our sins, hath quickened us together with Christ, (by grace ye are saved).

Amplified Version - (Ephesians 2:1-5), And you [He made alive], when you were dead [slain] by [your] trespasses and sins. (2), In which at one time you walked habitually. You were following the course and fashion of this world - were under the sway of the tendency of this present age - following the prince of the power of the air. (You were obedient to him and were under his control,) the [demon] spirit that still constantly works in the sons of disobedience - the careless, the rebellious and the unbelieving, who go against the purposes of God. (3), Among these we as well as you once lived and conducted ourselves in the passions of our flesh - our behavior governed by our corrupt and sensual nature; obeying the impulses of the flesh and the thoughts of the mind - our cravings dictated by our senses and our dark imaginings. We were then by nature children of [God's] wrath and heirs of [His] indignation, like the rest of mankind. (4), But God! So rich is He in His mercy! Because of and in order to satisfy the great and wonderful and intense love with which He loved us, (5), Even when we were dead slain by [our own] shortcomings and trespasses, He made us alive together in fellowship and in union with Christ. He gave us the very life of Christ Himself, the same new life with which He quickened Him. [For] it is by grace - by His favor and mercy which you did not deserve that you are saved (delivered from judgment and made partakers of Christ's salvation).

New American Standard Version - (Ephesians 2:1-5), And you were dead in your trespasses and sins, (2), in which you formerly walked according to the course of this world, according to the prince of the power of the air, of the spirit that is now working in the sons of disobedience. (3), Among them we too all formerly lived in the lusts of our flesh, indulging the desires of the flesh and of the mind, and were by nature children of wrath, even as the rest. (4), But God, being rich in mercy, because of His great love with which He loved us, (5), even when we were dead in our transgressions, made us alive together with Christ (by grace you have been saved).

New International Version - (Ephesians 2:1-5), As for you, you were dead in your transgressions and sins, (2), in which you used to live when you followed the ways of this world and of the ruler of the kingdom of the air, the spirit who is now at work in those who are disobedient. (3), All of us also lived among them at one time, gratifying the cravings of our sinful nature and following its desires and thoughts. Like the rest, we were by nature objects of wrath. (4), But because of His great love for us. God, who is rich in mercy, (5), made us alive with Christ even when we were dead in transgressions - it is by grace you have been saved.

Chapter 9

God's Plan for You

G od has created you to be His son or His daughter. He has predestined you from the beginning to be conformed inwardly (in character), to the image of His first borne Son who is Jesus Christ. God did this in order to prepare you as a member of His family. The bible reveals this in Romans 8:29 below.

King James Version - (Romans 8:29), For whom He did foreknow, He also did predestinate to be conformed to the image of His Son, that He might be the firstborn among many brethren.

Amplified Version - (Romans 8:29), For those whom He foreknew - of whom He was aware and loved beforehand - He also destined from the beginning (foreordaining them) to be molded into the image of His Son [and share inwardly His likeness], that He might become the first-born among many brethren.

New American Standard Version - (Romans 8:29), For whom He foreknew, He also predestined to be conformed to the image of His Son, that He might be the first-born among many brethren.

New International Version - (Romans 8:29), For those God foreknew He also predestined to be conformed to the likeness of His Son, that He might be the firstborn among many brothers.

God's plan also includes revealing things to you through the Holy Spirit who God places in you for this purpose. This is revealed for you in (1 Corinthians 2:10-14) of the bible below.

King James Version - (1 Corinthians 2:10-14), But God hath revealed them unto us by His Spirit: for the Spirit sear-cheth all things, yea, the deep things of God. (11), For what man knoweth the things of man, save the spirit of man which is in him? even so the things of God knoweth no man, but the Spirit of God. (12), Now we have received, not the spirit of the world, but the spirit which is of God; that we might know the things that are freely given to us of God. (13), Which things also we speak, not in the words which man's wisdom teacheth, but which the Holy Ghost teacheth; comparing spiritual things with spiritual. (14), But the natural man receiveth not the things of the Spirit of God: for they are foolishness unto him: neither can he know them, because they are spiritually discerned.

Amplified Version - (1 Corinthians 2:10-14), Yet to us God has unveiled and revealed them by and through His Spirit, for the (Holy) Spirit searches diligently, exploring and examining everything, even sounding the profound and bottomless things of God - the divine counsels and things hidden and beyond man's scrutiny. (11), For what person perceives (knows and understands) what passes through a man's thoughts except the man's own spirit within him? Just so, no one discerns (comes to know and comprehend) the thoughts of God except *the spirit of God. (12), Now we have not received the spirit (that belongs to) the world, but the (Holy) Spirit Who is from God, [given to us] that we might realize and comprehend and appreciate the gifts (of divine favor and blessings so freely and lavishly) bestowed on us by God. (13), And we are setting these truths forth in words not taught by human wisdom but taught by the (Holy) Spirit, combining and interpreting spiritual truths with spiritual language [to those who possess the (Holy) Spirit]. (14), But the natural, non-spiritual man does not accept or welcome or admit into his heart the gifts and teachings and revelations of the Spirit of God, for they are folly (meaningless nonsense) to him; and he is incapable of knowing them - of progressively recognizing, understanding and becoming better acquainted with them - because they are spiritually discerned and estimated and appreciated.*

New American Standard Version - (1 Corinthians 2:10-14), For to us God revealed them through the Spirit; for the Spirit searches all things, even the depths of God. (11), for who among men knows the thoughts of a man except the spirit of the man, which is in him? Even so the thoughts of God no one knows except the Spirit of God. (12), Now we have received, not the spirit of the world, but the Spirit Who is from God, that we might know the things freely given to us by God, (13), which things we also speak, not in words taught by human wisdom, but in those taught by the Spirit, combining spiritual thoughts with spiritual words. (14), But a natural man does not accept the things of the Spirit of God;

for they are foolishness to him, and he cannot understand them, because they are spiritually appraised.

New International Version - (1 Corinthians 2:10-14), but God has revealed it to us by His Spirit. The Spirit searches all things, even the deep things of God. (11), For who among men knows the thoughts of a man except the man's spirit within him? In the same way no one knows the thoughts of God except the Spirit of God. (12), We have not received the spirit of the world but the Spirit Who is from God, that we may understand what God has freely given us. (13), This is what we speak, not in words taught us by human wisdom but in words taught by the Spirit, expressing spiritual truths in spiritual words. (14), The man without the Spirit does not accept the things that come from the Spirit of God, for they are foolishness to him, and he cannot understand them, because they are spiritually discerned.

The bible reveals another important part of God's plan for you in (2 Corinthians 5:21) below. It clearly reveals that Jesus Christ took away your sin by giving His life in the place of yours on the cross as payment for your sins. This part of God's plan allows you to reestablish your relationship with God and be seen by Him as having His righteousness.

King James Version - (2 Corinthians 5:21), For He hath made Him to be sin for us, who knew no sin; that we might be made the righteousness of God in Him.

Amplified Version - (2 Corinthians 5:21), For our sake He made Christ [virtually] to be sin Who knew no sin, so that in and through Him we might become [endued with, viewed as in and examples of] the righteousness of God - what we ought to be, approved and accepted and in right relationship with Him, by His goodness.

New American Standard Version - (2 Corinthians 5:21), He made Him who knew no sin to be sin on our behalf, that we might become the righteousness of God in Him.

New International Version - (2 Corinthians 5:21), God made Him who had no sin to be sin for us, so that in Him we might become the righteousness of God.

The Amplified Version of (Romans 8:28) below, reveals that God is a partner in our labor, and that all things are fitted into God's plan for the good of those who love Him.

Amplified Version - (Romans 8:28), We are assured and know that [God being a partner in their labor], all things work together and are [fitted into a plan] for good to those who love God and are called according to [His] design and purpose.

In the Amplified Version of (Romans 8:29) below, it says (and share inwardly His likeness), this is referring to the inward likeness or the inward character of Christ. This verse is revealing to you that God put you here to develop the character of Christ in you. This character development will occur through the test and trials that you will encounter. It clearly reveals why you are here, and what God's plan is for you. You were predestined to be God's son or daughter before you were even borne, and you are here to develop the character of Christ.

Amplified Version - (Romans 8:29), For those whom He foreknew -of whom He was aware and loved beforehand - He also destined from the beginning (foreordaining them) to be molded into the image of His Son [and share inwardly His likeness], that He might become the first-born among many brethren.

The choice that you must make in order for God to accomplish His plan in your life, is to accept Jesus Christ as your personal Lord and Savior. In order to be saved from the penalty of your sins, you must accept Jesus Christ as your personal Lord and Savior, and turn away from a sinful life.

God wants everyone to be saved. The reason that you are here, is to give you an opportunity to be saved by accepting Christ as your Savior, and become a member of God's family. God is allowing you to make your own choice to do that, by giving you a free will and allowing you to choose. There is only one way to be saved from the judgment of your sins and enjoy eternal life with God and Jesus in heaven. The bible reveals in (Acts 4:12) below, that the only way to be saved and filled with the Holy Spirit is through Jesus Christ.

King James Version - (Acts 4:12), Neither is there salvation in any other: for there is none other name under heaven given among men, whereby we must be saved.

Amplified Version - (Acts 4:12), And there is salvation in and through no one else, for there is no other name under heaven given among men by and in which we must be saved.

New American Standard Version - (Acts 4:12), "And there is salvation in no one else; for there is no other name under heaven that has been given among men, by which we must be saved."

New International Version - (Acts 4:12), "Salvation is found in no one else, for there is no other name under heaven given to men by which we must be saved."

If you want to believe that Jesus died on the cross for you, and that His sacrifice actually paid the price for the sins in your life, ask God in prayer to help you to believe, and to have faith. I promise you He will. Even your faith is a gift from God.

I would like to close this chapter by restating God's plan for you. God created you and predestined you to be His son or His daughter, and He has set many principles in place to assure your spiritual growth and character development while you are here on earth. He did not just drop you off here and forget about you. He has placed His Holy Spirit in those of you who have chosen to accept Jesus as your personal Lord and Savior, to guide you from within. God is doing this for you because you are His child. God is creating His family here on earth right now, and you are a part of that family. He loves you very much, but many of you are completely unaware of it.

Don't be distracted by the circumstances in your life right now. Start living according to who you actually are.

You are God's son or His daughter. Don't be concerned with whether or not other people are able to recognize you for who you really are, because they didn't recognize Jesus either when He was here. When you need help, ask God in prayer to intervene in your situation and to help and guide you. You are God's child, and He will intervene in the circumstances in your life, but you have to ask.

Chapter 10

God is about to glorify you to all Creation

I still remember the day that I was being led by the Holy Spirit to reveal your coming glory to you in this chapter. I was very unsure about doing this because I knew that the devil and the demons were cast out of heaven for wanting the glory that belongs only to God. I was finally made aware of the glory that I was supposed to reveal to you in this chapter. The glory pertaining to you is clearly revealed in the Amplified version of (Romans 8:18,19) below. In verse 18, the bible refers to the glory that is about to be conferred on us, and in verse 19, it reveals that you will receive this glory when it is finally revealed to all creation that you are God's son or His daughter. I will include other versions of this verse for you below as well.

Amplified Version - (Romans 8:18,19), (18), [But what of that?] For I consider that the sufferings of this present time (this present life) are not worth being compared with the glory that is about to be revealed to us and in us and for us, and conferred on us! (19), For (even the whole) creation (all nature) waits expectantly and longs earnestly for God's sons to be made known - waits for the revealing, the disclosing of their sonship.

New American Standard Version - (Romans 8:18,19), (18), for I consider that the sufferings of this present time are not worthy to be compared with the glory that is about to be revealed to us. (19), For the anxious longing of the creation waits eagerly for the revealing of the sons of God.

New International Version - (Romans 8:18,19), (18), I consider that our present sufferings are not worth comparing with the glory that will be revealed in us. (19), The creation waits in eager expectation for the sons of God to be revealed.

King James Version - (Romans 8:18,19), (18), for I reckon that the sufferings of this present time are not worthy to be compared with the glory that shall be revealed in us. (19), for the earnest expectation of the creature waited for the manifestation of the sons of God.

Chapter 11

What God wants from You Today

What God wants from you today is a daily relationship with you. He is no different than any loving
father. He wants you as His child to come to Him in daily
prayer to nourish that Father and child relationship. The full
extent of this relationship remains an obscure biblical mys-
tery, but it will be revealed to you in this book. Any healthy
relationship requires communication between both of the
people in the relationship. Your relationship with God is no
different. In (Isaiah 58:9) below, the bible reveals that your
relationship with God actually involves communication to
you, as well as from you. This verse reveals that in response
to fasting and prayers the Lord will not only hear you, He
will also answer you. That is the relationship that God has
established with you today.

King James version - (Isaiah 58:9), Then shall thou call, and the Lord shall answer; thou shalt cry, and He shall say, "Here I am."

Amplified Version - (Isaiah 58:9), Then you shall call, and the Lord will answer; you shall cry, and He will say, "Here I am."

New American Standard Version - (Isaiah 58:9), Then you will call, and the Lord will answer, you will cry, and He will say, "Here I am."

New International Version - (Isaiah 58:9), Then you will call, and the Lord will answer; you will cry for help, and He will say: "Here am I."

It is also reveals to you in (Acts 13:1-4) below, that God answered Barnabas, Simeon, Lucius, Manaen and Saul through the Holy Spirit in response to their worshiping Him with fasting and prayer in the Church at Antioch.

King James Version - (Acts 13:1-4), (1), Now there were in the church that was at Antioch certain profits and teachers; as Barnabas, and Simeon that was called Niger, and Lucius of Cyrene, and Manaen, which had been brought up with Herod the tetrarch, and Saul. (2), As they ministered to the Lord, and fasted, the Holy Ghost said, "Separate Me Barnabas and Saul for the work whereunto I have called them." (3), And when they had fasted and prayed, and laid their hands on them, they sent them away. (4), So they, being sent forth by the Holy Ghost, departed unto Seleucia; and from thence they sailed to Cyprus.

Amplified Version - (Acts 13:1-4), (1), Now in the church (assembly) at Antioch there were prophets - inspired inter- preters of the will and purposes of God - and teachers, Barnabas, Symeon who was called Niger [black], Lucius of Cyrene, Manaen a member of the court of Herod the tettarch, and Saul. (2), While they were worshipping the Lord and fasting, the Holy Spirit said, "Separate now for Me Barnabas and Saul for the work to which I have called them." (3), Then after fasting and praying they put their hands on them and sent them away. (4), So then, being sent out by the Holy Spirit, they went down to Seleucia, and from [that port] they sailed away to Cyprus.

New American Standard Version - (Acts 13:1-4), (1), Now there were at Antioch, in the church that was there, prophets and teachers: Barnabas, and Simeon who was called Niger, and Lucius of Cyrene, and Manaen who had been brought up with Herod the tetrarch, and Saul. (2), And while they were ministering to the Lord and fasting, the Holy Spirit said "Set apart for Me Barnabas and Saul for the work to which I have called them." (3), Then, when they had fasted and prayed and laid their hands on them, they sent them away. (4), So, being sent out by the Holy Spirit, they went down to Seleucia and from there they sailed to Cyprus.

New International Version - (Acts 13:1-4), (1), In the church at Antioch there were prophets and teachers: Barnabas, Simeon called Niger, Lucius of Cyrene, Manaen (who had been brought up with Herod the tetrarch) and Saul. (2), While they were worshiping the Lord and fasting, the Holy Spirit said, "Set apart for Me Barnabas and Saul for the work to which I have called them." (3), So after they had fasted and prayed, they placed their hands on them and sent them off. (4), The two of them, sent on their way by the Holy Spirit, went down to Seleucia and sailed from there to Cyprus.

The bible reveals to you in (James 4:8) below, that when you draw near to God, He will draw near to you. This is what the prophets and teachers did in the Church at Antioch, when they worshiped God while they were fasting and praying, and God answered them.

King James Version (James 4:8), Draw nigh to God, and He will draw nigh to you. Cleanse your hands, ye sinners; and purify your hearts, ye double minded.

Amplified Version - (James 4:8), Come close to God and He will come close to you [Recognize that you are] sinners, get your soiled hands clean; [realize that you have been disloyal] wavering individuals with divided interests, and purify your hearts [of your spiritual adultery].

New American Standard Version - (James 4:8), Draw near to God and He will draw near to you. Cleanse your hands, you sinners; and purify your hearts, you double-minded.

New International Version - (James 4:8), Come near to God and He will come near to you. Wash your hands, you sinners, and purify your hearts, you double-minded.

In (1 Corinthians 2:10-12) below, the bible teaches us that God will reveal things to us through His indwelling Holy Spirit which He places in us for that purpose, so that we might know the things that are freely given to us by God. This verse clearly reveals that God will, and does reveal things to us through the indwelling Holy Spirit.

King James Version - (1 Corinthians 2:10-12), (10), But God has revealed them unto us by His Spirit: for the Spirit searcheth all things, yea, the deep things of God. (11), For what man knoweth the things of man, save the spirit of man which is in him? Even so the things of God knoweth no man, but the Spirit of God. (12), Now we have received, not the spirit of the world, but the Spirit which is of God; that we might know the things that are freely given to us of God. (13), Which things also we speak, not in the words which man's wisdom teaches, but which the Holy Ghost teaches; comparing spiritual things with spiritual. (14), but the natural man receiveth not the things of the Spirit of God: for they are foolishness unto him: neither can he know them, because they are spiritually discerned.

Amplified Version - (1 Corinthians 2:10-12), (10), Yet to us God has unveiled and revealed them by and through the Holy Spirit, for the (Holy) Spirit searches diligently, exploring and examining everything, even sounding the profound and bottom-less things of God - the divine counsels and things hidden and beyond man's scrutiny. (11), For what person perceives (knows and understands) what passes through a man's thoughts except the man's own Spirit within him? Just so no one discerns (comes to know and compre-hend) the thoughts of God except the Spirit of God. (12), Now we have not received the spirit (that belongs to) the world, but the (Holy) Spirit who is from God, [given to us] that we might realize and comprehend and appreciate the gifts (of divine favor and blessing so freely and lavishly) bestowed on us by God.

New American Standard Version - (1 Corinthians 2:10-12), (10), For to us God revealed them through the Spirit; for the Spirit searches all things, even the depths of God. (11), For who among men knows the thoughts of a man except the spirit of the man, which is in him? Even so the thoughts of God no one knows except the Spirit of God. (12), Now we have received, not the spirit of the world, but the Spirit Who is from God, that we might know the things freely given to us by God.

New International Version - (1 Corinthians 2:10-12), (10), but God had revealed it to us by His Spirit. The Spirit searches all things, even the deep things of God. (11), For who among men knows the thoughts of a man except the man's spirit within him? In the same way no one knows the thoughts of God except the Spirit of God. (12), We have not received the spirit of the world but the Spirit Who is from God, that we may understand what God has freely given us.

In order to reveal things to us, the Holy Spirit has to communicate with us. The Holy Spirit is basically a Spirit within us that God uses to communicate with us. In the Amplified Version of the bible in (John 16: 13-15) below, it clearly reveals that the Holy Spirit within us, will tell us what He hears from God. This is how God talks with us today. This is not a misprint, I just want to repeat this again for emphasis for those speed readers out there who have just blown by this very important revelation. This is how God talks with us today, through the Holy Spirit within us.

King James Version - (John 16:13-15), (13), "Howbeit when He, the Spirit of truth, is come, He will guide you into all truth; for He shall not speak of Himself; but whatsoever He shall hear, that shall He speak: He will show you things to come. (14), He shall glorify Me: for He shall receive of mine, and shall show it unto you. (15), All things that the Father hath are mine: therefore said I, that He shall take of mine, and shall show it unto you."

Amplified Version - (John 16:13-15), (13), "But when He, the Spirit of Truth (the truth-giving Spirit) comes, He will guide you into all truth - the whole, full truth. For He will not speak His own message - on His own authority - but He will tell whatever He hears [from the Father, He will give the message that has been given to Him] and He will announce and declare to you the things that are to come - that will happen in the future. (14), He will honor and glorify Me, because He will take of (receive, draw upon) what is Mine and will receive (declare, disclose, transmit) it to you. (15), Everything that the Father has in Mine. That is what I meant when I said that He will take the things that are Mine and will reveal (declare, disclose, transmit) them to you."

New American Standard Version - (John 16:13-15), (13), "But when He, the Spirit of truth, comes, He will guide you into all the truth; for He will not speak on His own initiative, but whatever He hears, He will speak; and He will disclose to you what is to come. (14), He shall glorify Me; for He shall take of Mine, and disclose it to you. (15), All things the Father has are Mine; therefore I said, that He takes of Mine, and will disclose it to you."

New International version - (John 16:13-15), (13), "But when He, the Spirit of truth, comes, He will guide you into all truth. He will not speak on His own; He will speak only what He hears, and He will tell you what is to come. (14),

He will bring glory to Me by taking from what is Mine and making it known to you. (15), All that belongs to the Father is mine. That is why I said the Spirit will take from what is Mine and make it known to you."

When you do talk with God in prayer each day, talk with Him in the same loving way that you would talk with your father here on earth. Remember, God is also your Father even though He is in heaven and you are here on earth right now. This won't always be the case.

Chapter 12

God Loves and Watches over You

✳

In the bible, God actually assures you that if anyone hurts you, or tries to corrupt you, or tries to destroy you, He will hurt them or destroy them. The reason behind this protective behavior is because you are God's child, and you are under His divine protection. God sees you as holy and sacred to Him, and in (1 Corinthians 3:16,17) below, the bible reveals to you that you are the temple of God, as the direct result of His Spirit dwelling in you.

King James Version - (1 Corinthians 3:16,17), Know ye not that ye are the temple of God, and that the Spirit of God dwelleth in you? (17), If any man defiles the temple of God, him shall God destroy; for the temple of God is holy, which temple ye are.

Amplified version - (1 Corinthians 3:16,17), Do you not discern and understand that you are God's temple (His sanctuary), and that God's Spirit has His permanent dwelling in you - to be at home in you. (17), If anyone does hurt to God's temple or corrupts [it with false doctrines] or destroys it, God will do hurt to him and bring him to the corruption of death and destroy him. For the temple of God is holy - sacred to Him - and that [temple] you [the believing church and its individual believers] are.

New American Standard Version - (1 Corinthians 3:16,17), Do you not know that you are a temple of God, and that the Spirit of God dwells in you? (17), If any man destroys the temple of God, God will destroy him, for the temple of God is holy, and that is what you are.

New International Version - (1 Corinthians 3:16,17), Don't you know that you yourselves are God's temple and that God's Spirit lives in you? (17), If anyone destroys God's temple, God will destroy him; for God's temple is sacred, and you are that temple.

In (Psalms 91:9-11) below, the bible reveals that God has assigned His angels to watch over you, to accompany you through this life, and to defend and preserve you in your walk with Him while you are here on earth. If you have accepted Jesus Christ as your Lord and Savior, God's angels are watching over you right now.

King James Version - (Psalms 91:9-11), Because thou hast made the Lord, which is My refuge, even the most High, thy habitation; (10), There shall no evil befall thee, neither shall any plague come nigh thy dwelling. (11), For He shall give His angels charge over thee, to keep thee in all thy ways.

Amplified Version - (Psalms 91:9-11), Because you have made the Lord your refuge, and the Most High your dwelling place, (10), There shall no evil befall you, nor any plague or calamity come near your tent. (11), For He will give His angels [especial] charge over you, to accompany and defend and preserve you in all your ways [of obedience and service].

New American Standard Version - (Psalms 91:9-11), For you have made the Lord, My refuge, even the Most High, your dwelling place. (10), No evil will befall you, nor will any plague come near your tent. (11), For He will give His angels charge concerning you, to guard you in all your ways.

New International Version - (Psalms 91:9-11), If you make the Most High your dwelling - even the Lord, who is my refuge - (10), then no harm will befall you, no disaster will come near your tent. (11), For He will command His angels concerning you to guard you in all your ways;

God has assigned a specific angel of the Lord to watch over just you, and this angel's only job is to watch over and to protect you while you are here on earth. This angel is commonly referred to by Christians today as their guardian angel. In the Amplified Version of the bible below, (Palms 34:7), says (the angel of the Lord). The word (the) in this verse is referring to one specific angel. It also says in this verse, (each of them He delivers). The word (each), in this verse is also a reference to only one individual person. In essence, this verse is revealing to you that God assigns an angel specifically to you, and also to each of the other Christians as well.

Amplified Version - (Psalms 34:7), The angel of the Lord encamps around those who fear Him - who revere and worship Him with awe; and each of them He delivers.

Chapter 13

Fasting and Prayer

Fasting is something that I had no personal experience with prior to writing this book for you. The bible reveals to you in (Isaiah 58:1-9) below, that when you fast and pray according to the bible, the Lord will not only hear you, but he will also answer you.

King James Version - (Isaiah 58:1-9), Cry aloud, spare not, lift up thy voice like a trumpet, and show my people their transgression, and the house of Jacob their sins. (2), Yet they seek Me daily, and delight to know My ways, as a nation that did righteousness, and forsook not the ordinance of their God: they ask of Me the ordinances of justice; they take delight in approaching to God. (3), Wherefore have we fasted, say they, and thou seest not? wherefore have we afflicted our soul, and thou takest no knowledge? Behold, in the day of your fast ye find pleasure, and exact all your labors. (4), Behold, ye fast for strife and debate, and to smite with the fist of wickedness: ye shall not fast as ye do this day, to make your voice to be heard on high. (5), Is it such a fast that I have chosen? a day for a man to afflict his soul? is it to bow down his head as a bulrush, and to spread sackcloth and ashes under him? wilt thou call this a fast, and an acceptable day to the Lord? (6), Is not this the fast that I have chosen? to loose the bands of wickedness, to undo the heavy burdens, and to let the oppressed go free, and that ye break every yoke? (7), Is it not to deal thy bread to the hungry, and that thou bring the poor that are cast out to thy house? when thou seest the naked, that thou cover him; and that thou hide not thyself from thine own flesh? (8), Then shall thy light break forth as the morning, and thine health shall spring forth speedily: and thy righteousness shall go before thee; the glory of the Lord shall be thy reward. (9), Then shall thou call, and the Lord shall answer; thou shalt cry, and He shall say, "Here I am."

Amplified Version - (Isaiah 58:1-9), Cry aloud, spare not, lift up your voice like a trumpet and declare to My people their transgressions, and to the house of Jacob their sins! (2), Yet they seek, inquire for and require Me daily, and delight [externally] to know My ways; as [if they were in reality] a nation that did righteousness and forsook not the ordinance of their God, they ask of Me righteous judgments; they delight to draw near to God [in visible ways]. (3), Why have we fasted, they say, and you do not see it? Why have we afflicted ourselves, and You take no knowledge of it? Behold, O Israel, in the day of your fast [when you should be grieving for your sins] you find business profit, and [instead of stopping all work, as the Law implies you and your workmen should] you extort from your hired servants a full amount of labor. (4), [The facts are] you fast only for strife and debate and to smite with the fist of wickedness. Fasting as you do today will not cause your voice to be heard on high. (5), Is such a fast as yours what I have chosen, a day for a man to humble himself with soul-sorrow? [Is true fasting merely mechanical?] Is it only to bow down his head like a bulrush, and to spread sackcloth and ashes under him [to indicate a condition of heart that he does not have]? Will you call this a fast and an acceptable day to the Lord? (6), [Rather,] is not this the fast that I have chosen; to loose the bonds of wickedness, to undo the bands of the yoke, to let the oppressed go free, and that you break every [enslaving] yoke? (7), Is it not to divide your bread with the hungry, and bring the home-less poor into your house? When you see the naked that you cover him, and that you hide not yourself from [the needs of] your own flesh and blood? (8), Then shall your light break forth as the morning, and your healing [your restoration and the power of a new life] shall spring forth speedily; your righteousness [your rightness, your justice and your right relationship with God] shall go before you [conducting you to peace and prosperity], and the glory of the Lord shall be your rear guard. (9), Then you shall call, and the Lord will answer; you will cry, and He will say, "Here I am."

New American Standard Version - (Isaiah 58:1-9), Cry loudly, do not hold back; raise your voice like a trumpet, and declare to my people their transgressions, and to the house of Jacob their sins. (2), "Yet they seek Me day by day, and delight to know My ways, as a nation that has done righ-teousness, and has not forsaken the ordinance of their God. They ask Me for just decisions. They delight in the nearness of God. (3), Why have we fasted and Thou dost not notice? behold, on the day of your fast you find your desire, and drive hard all your workers. (4), Behold, you fast for conten-tion and strife and to strike with a wicked fist. You do not fast like you do today to make your voice heard on high.

(5), "Is it a fast like this which I choose, a day for a man to humble himself? Is it for bowing one's head like a reed, and for spreading out sackcloth and ashes as a bed? Will you call this a fast, even an acceptable day to the Lord? (6), Is this not the fast which I choose, to loosen the bonds of wickedness, to undo the bands of the yoke, and to let the oppressed go free, and break every yoke? (7), Is it not to divide your bread with the hungry, and bring the homeless poor into the house; when you see the naked, to cover him; and not to hide yourself from your own flesh? (8), Then your light will break out like the dawn, and your recovery will speedily spring forth; and your righteousness will go before you; The glory of the Lord will be your rear guard. (9), Then you will call, and the Lord will answer; you will cry, and He will say, "Here I am."

New International Version - (Isaiah 58:1-9), Shout it aloud, do not hold back, raise your voice like a trumpet. Declare to My people their rebellion and to the house of Jacob their sins. (2), For day after day they seek Me out; they seem eager to know my ways, as if they were a nation that does what is right and has not forsaken the commands of its God. They ask Me for just decisions and seem eager for God to come near them. (3), Why have we fasted, they say, and you have not seen it? Why have we humbled ourselves, and you have not noticed? Yet on the day of your fasting, you do as you please and exploit all your workers. (4), Your fasting ends in quarreling and strife, and in striking each other with wicked fists. You cannot fast as you do today and expect you voice to be heard on high. (5), Is this the kind of fast I have chosen, only a day for a man to humble himself? Is it only for bowing one's head like a reed and for lying on sackcloth and ashes? Is that what you call a fast, a day acceptable to the Lord? (6), Is not this the kind of fasting I have chosen: to loose the chains of injustice and untie the cords of the yoke, to set the oppressed free and break every yoke? (7), Is it not to share your food with the hungry and to provide the poor wanderer with shelter - when you see the naked, to clothe him, and not to turn away from your own flesh and blood? (8), Then your light will break forth like the dawn, and your healing will quickly appear; then your righteousness will go before you, and the glory of the Lord will be your rear guard. (9), Then you will call, and the Lord will answer; you will cry for help, and He will say: "Here am I."

When I read verse (9), of (Isaiah 58:1-9), I wasn't sure it was even possible. It was only after reading four different versions of these verses several times that I understood what these bible verses were revealing. The simple truth revealed here is that the Lord will in fact answer you when you fast and pray. Prior to reading this verse, I was not aware of this promise in the bible. I have to admit that I was skeptical as to its validity. In response to my skepticism, I searched in my bible to find out who wrote this verse. I discovered that a prophet named Isaiah wrote it. Isaiah was actually a prophet of the Lord's who lived in Jerusalem. Isaiah made accurate prophecies about events that occurred more than a hundred years after his death, and some that apply to our day as well. Now, I had discovered who wrote this verse, and that he was a real prophet who has a lot of creditability. I was still having a lot of trouble actually believing the part of this verse that claims that the Lord will answer us when we fast and pray according to the bible. I feel bad about not instantly believing what the bible was clearly revealing to me in this verse, but I had not been made aware of this revelation about praying while fasting before. I was not convinced that in response to fasting and praying that the Lord would answer us. In order to prove to myself that this does actually happen, I immediately started looking for a documented case of it happening to someone in the bible. Since the bible clearly reveals that the Lord will answer you, I wanted to find out if He had answered anyone in the past. In an attempt to uncover this information, I began my search through the bible for proof.

I found my proof in (Acts 13:2,3), of the bible. It says that while they were worshiping the Lord and fasting, the Holy Spirit said, "Set apart for me Barnabas and Saul for the work to which I have called them." and after they had fasted and prayed, they placed their hands on them and sent them off.

These obscure biblical truths reveal that the Lord will answer you when you fast and pray, and that He has done it in the past as recorded in (acts 13:2,3), of the bible.

I want to point out another very important fact that is being revealed to you in (Acts 13:2,3). God is revealing to you that the Holy Spirit is the one who spoke the words that were being conveyed by the Lord. This is a very important description of the communication between the Lord and you. The bible is revealing here that when God does answer you today, He will do it through the indwelling Holy Spirit, who He has placed in you for this purpose. You can read these revelations for yourself in (acts 13:2,3) below.

King James Version - (Acts 13:2,3), As they ministered to the Lord, and fasted, the Holy Ghost said, "Separate me Barnabas and Saul for the work whereunto I have called them." (3), And when they had fasted and prayed, and laid their hands on them, they sent them away.

Amplified Version - (Acts 13:2,3), While they were worshipping the Lord and fasting, the Holy Spirit said, "Separate now for Me Barnabas and Saul for the work to which I have called them." (3), Then after fasting and praying they put their hands on them and sent them away.

New American Standard Version - (Acts 13:2,3), And while they were ministering to the Lord and fasting, the Holy Spirit said, "Set apart for Me Barnabas and Saul for the work to which I have called them." (3), Then, when they had fasted and prayed and laid their hands on them, they sent them away.

New International Version - (Acts 13:2,3), While they were worshiping the Lord and fasting, the Holy Spirit said, "Set apart for me Barnabas and Saul for the work to which I have called them," (3), So after they had fasted and prayed, they placed their hands on them and sent them off.

Take the time to not only read, but to study the revelations in (Acts 13:2,3) above. They not only reveal to you that when you fast and pray the Lord will answer you, but they also reveal to you that He will answer you through the indwelling Holy Spirit. These two revelations are obscure biblical mysteries that should have a profound impact on the way that you communicate with God in the future.

Before I end this chapter on fasting, I want to disclose something of value that I discovered regarding fasting. I acknowledge and understand that the acceptable length of a fast today is forty days and forty nights. When I was introduced to fasting however, I was informed that God would even respond to you if you fast just one meal accompanied with prayer. I found this to be true. I now believe that God will acknowledge and respond to any fast that you come to Him with in prayer. After all, you are His child.

Closing Words from the Author

I would like to leave you with some profound statement, as most writers do. I leave you with this:

God is involved in your daily life in many ways that you may not be aware of right now. God reveals many of the ways that He does get involved in your life in the bible for you, but a lot of these have remained hidden for all practical purposes until now. This book has been written to reveal them to you. The bible reveals in (1 Corinthians 2:10-14), that we will receive the Holy Spirit who is from God, and that He will reveal God's secret wisdom to us. I have found this to be true. In (1 Corinthians 2:7), of your bible it refers specifically to God's secret wisdom, as a wisdom that has been hidden and that God has destined for our glory before time began. God's Revelations about you, reveals this infor-mation for you. The revelations in this book are being documented here for you in an effort to change your life, and prepare you for what is to come. I hope they achieve that noble purpose.